Skyways

DETECTIVE PLAY

Paul Groves

Nick Dick goes on TV

> *Cast*
> **Nick Dick**   **Voice**
> **Yvette**   **Caron**
> **Chief**   **Floor Manager**
> **Mark**   **Producer**

(A police station. The phone rings.)

Nick Dick: Nick Dick here.

Yvette: This is Blue Peter.

Nick Dick: Blue Peter?

Yvette: Yes, I'm Yvette. We'd like you to come on TV.

Nick Dick: What for?

Yvette: To tell us about the crimes you have solved.

Nick Dick: I'll have to ask the Chief.
Chief, they want me to go on Blue Peter.

Chief: Have they lost Bonnie?

Nick Dick: No, they want to know about some of the crimes I have solved.

Chief: You do that, Nick. It will be good for the police.

(A TV Studio.)

Yvette: Just sit there, Nick. When the red light goes on that camera you will know we are on air.

Nick Dick: Okay.

Yvette: Are you nervous?

Nick Dick: Just a bit.

Producer: Ready, Yvette?

Yvette: Yes, ready.

Producer: Five, four, three, two, one . . .

(Blue Peter music.)

Yvette: In the studio today we have the famous lady detective, Nick Dick.

Nick Dick: Hello.

Yvette: I'm glad you could take time off from solving crimes to be with us.

Nick Dick: I'm glad to be here.

Yvette: How many crimes have you solved, Nick?

Nick Dick: It must be over 500.

Yvette: Tell us about your most famous crime.

Nick Dick: That must be Lord Howard.

Yvette: Lord Howard?

Nick Dick: He was strangled by a strange night plant.

Yvette: A plant?

Nick Dick: Yes.

Yvette: How did you know that?

Nick Dick: I had a hunch.

Yvette: Tell me about your hunches.

Nick Dick: To be a detective you have to think things out.

Yvette: Yes.

Nick Dick: Lord Howard was not liked by the butler, his wife and his son.

Yvette: Yes.

Nick Dick: And he had just sacked the gardener.

Yvette: So anyone of them could have strangled him?

Nick Dick: Yes, but I saw a green mark on his neck, so I went into the conservatory at night with a knife.

Yvette: And the plant tried to strangle you?

Nick Dick: Yes, the gardener knew Lord Howard went into the conservatory at night to look at his plants before going to bed.

Yvette: You put yourself in danger, Nick.

Nick Dick: You have to, to be a detective.

Mark: Tell us about another crime. Which one puzzled you the most?

Nick Dick: That would be the crime of the gorilla and the jewels.

Mark: The gorilla and the jewels?

Nick Dick: Yes, a gorilla was stealing jewels at night.

Mark: How did you solve that?

Nick Dick: It was luck. I took my son to the circus.

Mark: The circus?

Nick Dick: Yes, I saw a clown on stilts and then I had my hunch.

Mark: What was your hunch?

Nick Dick: Well you see, the big footprints did not belong to a gorilla.

Mark: No.

Nick Dick: Then I found out that the clown had dressed up as a gorilla.

Mark: Another crime solved.

Nick Dick: Yes.

Caron: Tell me about the crime at the races.

Nick Dick: A jockey was shot dead.

Caron: I read about it.

Nick Dick: But we could find no gun. We searched everyone and everywhere.

Caron: They could have got out of the race track.

Nick Dick: No, the police stopped everyone. I looked at the film again and again to see if I could see anyone running.

Caron: And you did?

Nick Dick: No, but then I had a hunch. You see there was a wobble on the film.

Carole: A wobble?

Nick Dick: Yes, a good cameraman does not do that.

Caron: And you found a gun?

Nick Dick: Yes, in the camera.

Caron: I hope there's not one in that camera.

Nick Dick: I think I would have a hunch, if it did.

Caron: Why did the cameraman do it?

Nick Dick: He had a big bet on another horse.

Yvette: What crime was the best one you solved?

Nick Dick: That would be the one with the dolphins and the drugs.

Yvette: Why was that the best?

Nick Dick: Drugs can kill. I had to stop them getting in.

Yvette: Tell us about your hunch this time.

Nick Dick: Well, I saw the fishermen putting their nets into the sea and I saw something like a fish in them.

Yvette: Oh?

Nick Dick: Fishermen throw back fish they don't want. They don't put them back into the sea in nets.

Yvette: We are so pleased that you could come, Nick and now we are going to give you something.

(Floor Manager jumps onto the stage.)

Floor Manager: Not before I give her something.

Yvette: Oh!

Mark: What's going on?

Floor Manager: Keep back! You're going to get more than a Blue Peter badge, Nick. You're going to get a bullet.

Nick Dick: Are you mad? Who are you? What do you want with me?

Floor Manager: I am the chief of the smuggling gang. Those dolphins were my idea. You spoiled it all.

Nick Dick: You won't get away with this.

Floor Manager: I will. I will kill you and a helicopter will pick me up from the roof of the studio. Nick Dick will die.

Voice (*off stage*): No, she won't because she is not Nick Dick!

Floor Manager: Not Nick Dick?

Voice (*off stage*): No, I am Nick Dick and I have a gun pointed at you, so you can drop yours. Your helicopter is in police hands.

(Black out. Someone screams. Lights come back on.)

Voice: Are you all right?

Nick Dick: Yes, I'm okay.

(A TV Studio three days later.)

Yvette: I'm surprised you've come back, Nick. Are you the real Nick Dick?

Nick Dick: Yes, I am. I am this time.

Caron: You must have had a big hunch.

Nick Dick: Well, it wasn't a hunch. Someone told me about the Floor Manager being the chief of the smuggling gang.

Caron: What you would call a 'grass'?

Nick Dick: That's it. But I had no proof. So I had him followed.

Yvette: And he admitted he was the chief of the gang, here on TV for everyone to see.

Nick Dick: What better proof can you get?

Mark: Well, it's the most exciting thing that has ever happened on Blue Peter.

Caron: And this time we would like you to have . . .

Yvette and Mark: A Blue Peter badge.

Nick Dick: Can I have two?

Mark: Two?

Nick Dick: Yes, one for me and one for my double.